CW01082366

X

Twenty-Four Seven,

In my

feelings

VII

A.O.U

Intra Muse Collective

XXIV Twenty-Four Seven, in my feelings
VII © 2022

Avril

All rights reserved.

No part of this publication may be
reproduced, stored in a retrieval system,
or transmitted, in any form or by any
means, electronic, mechanical,
photocopying, recording or otherwise,
without the prior written permission of
the presenters.

Avril asserts the moral right to be
identified as the author of this work.

Presentation by *BookLeaf Publishing*

Web: www.bookleafpub.com

E-mail: info@bookleafpub.com

ISBN: 9789358364392

First edition 2022

For those who allow their mind to wander, whose imagination is limitless. For those who make sure love is a verb reflecting through their efforts and actions. For those who protect their peace and energy by any means necessary.

ACKNOWLEDGEMENT

Thanking BookLeaf Publishing for developing a challenge that has allowed me to share my poetry with you. Thanking God for providing opportunities and inspiration, allowing me to take advantage of them and create this piece of art. Big shout out to my sister, Ria, for being my sounding board, for the words of encouragement and improvement. Grateful for Nadia, my creative sistren, for the illustrations. Thanking the people and situations that have inspired these words. Lastly, I am thanking myself, I am so proud of you for taking part in this challenge. Look at what you have achieved, plenty more to come. Intra Muse Collective, soon reach.

1.

Yes

Deeper than touch

There is something about touching you

That keeps me calm

A slight movement of protection

Like a baby in your palm

No words are needed when we communicate in affection

I yearn for you to explode in my inner sanctum

Our body heat, a furnace

Your tongue down my throat

Delving deeper, exploring beyond the surface

Venturing into the unknown

The throbbing and thrusting

Overly anticipated

Electricity charged lusting

You feel it too

Yes, there is something about touching
you

2.

Fear Presents

I constantly evaluate my life

especially the failed attempts at success

Whether they be work, relationships,

or progress

I see sometimes things didn't work

but that was in my favour

more often than not,

I sense

fear was a factor

It didn't hide in the shadows of my mind

It presented itself like a cautionary
method

providing strategic pros and cons

My fear presents as logic, probability,
and prediction

Everything is black and white

and solutions easy, like a simple
equation

but life and scenarios aren't based on
statistics

Experiences breed informed decisions

But is opting out any way to live?

I harness the crippling fear and make it
the reason

why I live and not just exist.

3.

Not a 10, shun (Attention)

Do I have to be a 10

To get your attention?

You say you want a lady in the streets

A freak in the sheets

Long hair past her neck

No weave, baldness or extensions

She needs to be able to cook a 3 course meal

Give head like it's the only option on the menu

Wear next to nothing and still be classy

Takes all your shit and isn't sassy

She needs to be patient and passive

But passionate

Allow me to reintroduce the question

Do I have to be a 10, to get your attention?

From where we stand, you offer nothing

You take without the thought of giving

You require so much

But give less than anything worthwhile

You don't match my efforts or your own credentials

Your standards are high but what you're offering is futile

Are you even a 10, to be worthy of my attention?

4.

He wants, I want

He wants to:

Strum me like a guitar

Bang me like a drum

Netflix and chill, with all the goodies,

Then run

I want:

Amazon Prime and commitment

Making sweet hums to slow jams

Growing comfy in the winter months

And still date in the summertime

He wants:

Late night dirty pics

And little to no small talk

A quick bang when he's horny

And only lust filled phone calls

I want:

Sunday lunch with our parents

Matrimony, kids, and a mortgage

Constant forehead kisses

Honest and thoughtful conversations

We are both on different pages

A slow and recurring development

He wants Netflix and Chill

I want Amazon Prime and Commitment

5.

Fairy Tale Endings

Cinderella and Snow White

Got their happily ever after

We put our love on cruise control

What a disaster!

Being told you're not the one

So you've got to let them go

We thought we were the ones for this

Real Empire, Ride or Die

Cookie and Lucious

But the truth is...

If their love doesn't hold you,

then you've got to let them go.

6.

Risk

Like Icarus, I have flown too close to the sun and gotten burnt

Like Daedalus, I have flown too close to the sea and drowned

Risk taking is delving into the unknown

It's delicate

To strike whilst the iron is hot

Is always recommended

But to air on the side of caution produces a smarter, tactical advantage

Is it worth it?

7.

What is freedom?

To be naked amongst the clothed

To be unshackled around the enslaved

To speak loosely without the
consequence of a glossectomy

To view a glass ceiling as an attainable
opportunity

To not have to worry that your skin
colour makes you a target

To practice your religion and not be
associated with terrorism

To not have your reproductive rights
discussed like the weather, with
indifference

To not be killed for your sexuality or
gender identity

To be able to wear your natural hair or protective style without causing an uproar

To take the knee against injustice and not be booed

To love outside of your race and class and not constantly be demonised

To speak about your experiences and not receive eye rolls and sighs

To be free of judgement,

Carefree in life.

The freeing feeling of knowing

That freedom is more than just a state of mind.

8.

Focus

I imagine what I want

Therefore, my purpose is clear

I leap into the unknown

With nothing but faith getting me there

The depth of the sea is not my business

Neither is your doubt or hesitation

As I know where I want to be

The trees may rise to make a forest

And winding roads may make a maze

But nothing will distract me from my mission

I will choose to take the path less travelled

Because sometimes

Shortcuts are the long way

9.

The Person who did it

What an inconvenience

This dark abyss won't disappear

The fake joy is more forced action

Than its genuine manifestation

What an inconvenience

Another delay, unwelcomed at the end
of the day

All I wanted was to get home

The person making my journey longer

Displayed no fear and no hope

Ending their day

As another Londoner passes away

The person who did it

How selfish they are

How will their family feel and their peers adjust

To the once 3d image they saw

To a distant and distorted memory of the person they knew

Forgiveness is not an option

You delayed my journey

I've missed the shops

I can't buy my lotion

You should've spoken rather than taken it

The signs were there they will say

But everyone goes through hard times

No reason for your life to pay

The person who did it has found relief

Feeling free and at ease

You jumped and hope resumed

The end of misery and neglect

But you delayed my journey

Although I had nothing planned

Maybe if I'd taken more time

And asked about your well being

You'd still be around

I could have turned that frown gradually
upside down

But I was too wrapped up in things that
didn't matter

Although you are gone and are spoken
about in the past

The future can change for the better

A learning experience

As one we should gather and check in
on each other

Taking care of ourselves isn't selfish

It's a priority

Mentally, physically, emotionally, and spiritually

The person who did it is no longer amongst us

But a lesson can be learnt from their passing

And the horror of their absence

The person who did it, taught me that

10.

Demolition

Combating the fiends of the mind

requires constant work and positivity

Boxing myself out of depressive modes

Uppercut, right hook, dodge

Sometimes to attack is to give it power

Wrestling with emotions, that can't be
controlled

grappling with my feelings, a pained
ego, in a submissive hold

Karate my uncertainty and doubt,

with open handed chops breaking
through,

Capoeira with my inner demons, dance
with them,

outsmart, exhaust to destroy

I am in a constant MMA battle with myself,

I am my own worst enemy

My biggest critic

My worst opponent

I tear me down

Worse than anyone could

My enemy is disguised as my inner voice of reason

Gently coercing me into a state of demolition

11.

Beach Bids Thee A G'day

Surrounded by the tropics,

Eyes blinded by rays and beams

Skin soaking in the Vitamin D

Vibrant golden granules, inviting me
closer

As my soles brace for impact

The grains are absorbing heat

The burning sensation below my feet

Not a deterrent

But a needed encouragement

To make it to safety

Where the vast, blue, wavy quilt will
save me

One step at a time

As I approach this coastline

The tide greets me

Reaches out to engulf me

Up to my knees it eventually reaches

And leaves me with temporary relief

I am welcomed

12.

Life Remote

I wish time away

to skip to the good bits of life

to avoid the disappointment, sadness,
and strife

To fast forward the struggle

and mute the negativity

Repeatedly reverse and play

all the moments of happiness

Skip past all the self-doubt

and arrive at the celebrations

Get a synopsis for the next scene

decide whether to live it or not

Sadly life isn't controlled by a remote

where I can manipulate the plot

13.

Sober After Inspiration

I'm blowing trees

To make time go faster,

Make minutes pass quicker

Until you're back with me

Another injection of inspiration

Will ensure your presence within

I wait for that feeling

Only you unlocking my mind can bring

Another sniff of oxygen

Your absence causes me pain

Fighting temptation to catalyse the experience

With a Class A

Willing away time to feel close to you

Be next to you, be on you

For pleasures only you can provide

Without you my senses divide

I'm stuck in a vacuum without you near

You and I are the perfect pair

No other drug can compare to your influence

The hollow, intolerable emptiness

After such a fulfilling high

That brings more pleasure

Than all drugs combined

30

14.

Breast, Tits, Chest

My breasts, tits, chest

propelled me into adulthood

before the rest

of my body could

sweat, bleed, stretch

The woman, bless her, tried to battle
nature with a hot wooden spoon and a
West African procedure named Press

I began to view these extensions

as hindrances and distractions

the sudden unclipping of a bra

and the over emphasis of how bulgy
they were

against a pre-pubescent body

Running was no longer light sprightly

Instead, I felt weighed down

My breasts, chest, tits

we have come a long way

I now refer to them as the twins

rather than offensive extensions

I appreciate their use for production and
other functions

To serve life and body

Although our initial introduction was
complicated

and I felt betrayed by your presence

I thank you for standing tall

with some support and providing shape
in

bathing suits, tops and dresses

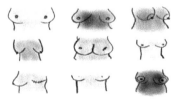

15.

Money

They say money is the root of all evil,

I have never heard money talk

Never seen it commit a crime

Betray a friend

Or be greedy

To others money is the answer to all their problems

Better health, better way of life

Better prospects for them and their family

Is money really the root of all evil

Or are humans always choosing the evil route?

16.

Michaela, Issa, Lena (Representation Matters)

You are amazing

Your art, craft, and talent unmatched

You have opened my eyes

To experience what would have been hidden

And circumstances that may never be uttered

Issa taught me there's no shame in being awkward and black

It's not an anomaly, and although growing pains can cause you to become Insecure

Work through it, as success lies beyond

Michaela let me laugh so hard, I choked on Chewing Gum

Whilst my mind pondered over how

I may destroy you, for day and nights to come.

Lena arrived like Shakespeare and presented

Queen and Slim a modern-day tragedy

Showing the depth of the devastation within a corrupt system

She then topped it with something most can relate

The madness, uncertainty and increasing feeling of failure and navigating our dreams whilst being in our Twenties

In a world that enjoys limiting the black cinematic experience to slavery and crime

Michaela, Issa, Lena et al have expanded the story lines,

An explorative experience, moving with the times.

17.

Continent

The abundance of resource

so blessed is this continent

but the corruption is rife

the gaping divide between the rich and poor

the limited opportunities for development

The struggle worn like a badge of honour

when in fact there is nothing to be proud of

The politicians only out to fill their own pockets

and profit from the disadvantage of others

A system not built to progress

Instead cause generational stress

What will be the straw that breaks the camel's back?

That forces positive change to be an agenda for a new age

How do we fight corruption, with an infrastructure not built for conversion?

with traditional beliefs not moving with the times

and forward-thinking treated like an abominable act

The youth want change

but trying to navigate an old boy's club requires status

and once in those places, those who wanted their nation to be elevated

have become part of the problem

enticed by rapacity

and driven by self-indulgence

Selling off the very thing that would make us contenders

and provide support for the people

but we are stuck in a never changing
cycle

18.

God, according to me

I am a believer

But my beliefs may differ

The way I practice and compose myself

May not be to your standards or understanding

I am not a finished product

I am constantly evolving, I know there are things beyond my understanding, that in fact no one can explain

Some religious people may think it is their right

To be judge, jury and executioner

For some, religious institutions and teachings are prisons

Forcing them to fold and be half of themselves

A reluctance to engage with God

Because of human critique

My God is energy, My God is a vibe

That you invite into your life

God is omnipresent

And accepting of all

God is whatever you need at the time

In the midst of chaos, God brings peace,

Within devastations and heartbreak,
God awakens your inner fighter

When you delight in surprise, success
and positive outcomes

God is cheering you on

I was informed that all of us are created
in God's image

So we must be perfect, but we have
also been granted free will

And although My God is energy and a vibe

To see real benefits

You must first invite God into your life

19.

In Music, I trust

You always welcome me with a warm embrace

You know all the right things to say

the chords to my heart

depending on my mood

You're like a warm summer's day accompanied by a gentle breeze

You are the tropical showers in a humid climate

you are my wellies in the snow

Although my ears experience you primarily

The rest of my senses

welcome your presence, even if it is secondary

to my initial needs

I speak the words in my ears from my
lips

holding a tune that emphasizes feelings
of more than bliss

sometimes it's sadness, pity, and hate

other times it's happiness, excitement
and elation

Sometimes you teach

and other times you're present just for
body movement

I see colours depicting your influence

and smell the intended feelings in the air

Sometimes my feet have no control and
my body just follows

Sometimes the words resonate and
cause the wetting of an eye

There are so many of you, that bring me
so much joy and nostalgia

Different genres, voices and power

48

storytelling and rhymes, a flow

Oh MUSIC, you have done more for me
than you will ever know

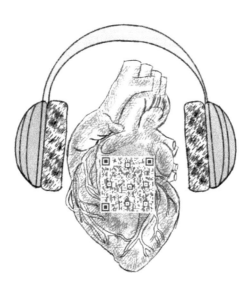

20.

Societal Express

There are fleeting statements

that we all say without a second thought

but the damage it can cause

can change the trajectory and course of someone's life.

Boys don't cry, now he is an emotionally stunted man, afraid to appear weak in any and under every circumstance

Girls are delicate and meek

now she avoids speaking her mind, so she won't be labelled bossy

and although she is strong, she must appear weak

Boys who like pink are deemed feminine, girls who like blue deemed unmanageable

The comments get wilder as they get older

struggling to find where they fit in

and why society's opinions

are so limiting

What has now been created

are kids with views that are not their own

judging others on things that they don't view as the norm

The boy now asks 'why are you such a cry baby?'

and the girl questions her own biology due to a colour or clothing

that sparks no joy

Boys and Girls

express yourselves

emotion is not weak

colours do not define you

dresses don't make you more of a girl

and crying doesn't make you any less of
a boy

Try and be accepting of all

The world is already way too
dysfunctional, do we really need more?

Milton Keynes UK
Ingram Content Group UK Ltd.
UKHW020750190424
441445UK00014B/598